D1093232

COUNTRY PROFILES

GUATEMALA

BY ALICIA Z. KLEPEIS

BLASTOFF!
DISCOVERY

BELLWETHER MEDIA • MINNEAPOLIS, MN

Blastoff! Discovery launches a new mission: reading to learn. Filled with facts and features, each book offers you an exciting new world to explore!

This edition first published in 2019 by Bellwether Media, Inc.

No part of this publication may be reproduced in whole or in part without written permission of the publisher.
For information regarding permission, write to Bellwether Media, Inc., Attention: Permissions Department, 6012 Blue Circle Drive, Minnetonka, MN 55343.

Library of Congress Cataloging-in-Publication Data

LC record for Guatemala available at:
  https://lccn.loc.gov/2018039876

Text copyright © 2019 by Bellwether Media, Inc. BLASTOFF! DISCOVERY and associated logos are trademarks and/or registered trademarks of Bellwether Media, Inc. SCHOLASTIC, CHILDREN'S PRESS, and associated logos are trademarks and/or registered trademarks of Scholastic Inc., 557 Broadway, New York, NY 10012.

Editor: Rebecca Sabelko   Designer: Brittany McIntosh

Printed in the United States of America, North M̶̶ ̶ ̶ ̶ ̶MN.

TABLE OF CONTENTS

LIBERTAD
15 DE
SEPTIEMBRE
DE 1821

THE GREAT PLAZA
TIKAL NATIONAL PARK

The sun shines through the jungle as a family arrives at Tikal National Park. Soon, the Great Plaza comes into view. Incredible stone temples rise 213 feet (65 meters) into the air! The kids love the Temple of the Giant Jaguar. Its many steps seem to stretch to the sky!

OTHER TOP SITES

LAKE ATITLÁN

PACAYA

PALACIO NACIONAL
(NATIONAL PALACE)

SEMUC CHAMPEY

As the day continues, the family wanders among Tikal's ruins. They encounter pyramids, stone figures, and 2,000-year-old carvings made by the **Maya** people. From atop one of the temples, the family hears the sounds of toucans. They spy spider monkeys leaping from tree to tree. Welcome to Guatemala!

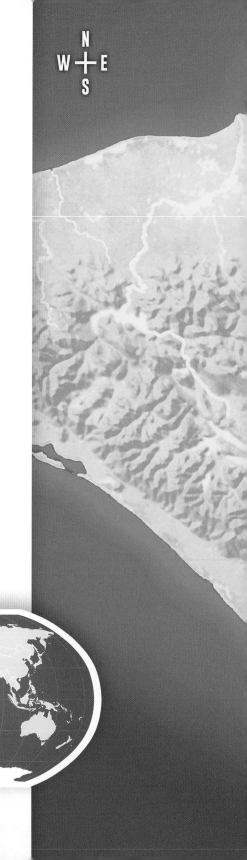

LOCATION

Guatemala is located in Central America. It covers 42,042 square miles (108,889 square kilometers) and is a little smaller than the state of Pennsylvania. Guatemala's capital, Guatemala City, is in the south-central part of the country.

To the west and north of Guatemala is the country of Mexico. Belize is Guatemala's eastern neighbor. The turquoise waters of the Caribbean Sea touch Guatemala on its small eastern coastline. Honduras and El Salvador border Guatemala to the southeast. The Pacific Ocean washes upon the southern shores.

BLACK SAND BEACHES

Beaches on Guatemala's Pacific coast have black sand. This sand forms when black volcanic rock breaks into smaller pieces.

MEXICO

BELIZE

CARIBBEAN
SEA

GUATEMALA

QUETZALTENANGO

GUATEMALA
CITY

MIXCO - - - ●

● - - - VILLA NUEVA

HONDURAS

PACIFIC
OCEAN

EL
SALVADOR

Northern Guatemala is covered by the forests and lakes of the Petén **Plateau**. The Cuchamatán Mountains span from the western highlands into the central highlands. Here, the Motagua River flows northeast into the **Gulf** of Honduras. The **volcanic** Sierra Madre Mountains stretch across the south. The Pacific lowlands are covered in farmland.

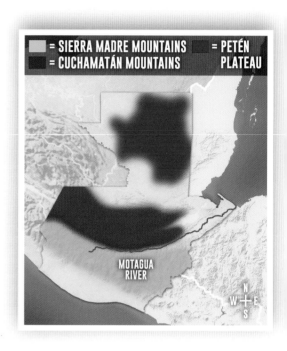

= SIERRA MADRE MOUNTAINS   = PETÉN PLATEAU
= CUCHAMATÁN MOUNTAINS

MOTAGUA RIVER

N W E S

ACTIVE VOLCANOES

Guatemala is home to over 30 volcanoes. In June 2018, an active volcano called Fuego erupted.

FUEGO

MOTAGUA RIVER

GUATEMALA CITY

Average seasonal highs and lows

JANUARY
HIGH: 72 °F (22 °C)
LOW: 55 °F (13 °C)

APRIL
HIGH: 78 °F (26 °C)
LOW: 60 °F (16 °C)

JULY
HIGH: 74 °F (23 °C)
LOW: 61 °F (16 °C)

OCTOBER
HIGH: 73 °F (23 °C)
LOW: 61 °F (16 °C)

°F = degrees Fahrenheit
°C = degrees Celsius

Guatemala ranges from hot and humid in the lowlands to dry in the central plateau. The dry season is from November to April. But **trade winds** bring rain all year long. Severe **tropical** storms are common in September and October.

WHITE-NOSED COATI

Guatemala's landscape is filled with wildlife. The Petén is home to white-nosed coatis that search for insects on the forest floor. Black-handed spider monkeys swing from tree to tree. Keel-billed toucans use their colorful bills to grab fruit. Fer-de-lance snakes slither about looking for prey. Quetzals struggle to find homes because many forests have been destroyed.

QUETZAL

Along the Pacific coast, green iguanas make their nests on the ground. They must look out for predators such as caimans. Many kinds of turtles swim in the ocean, too.

FER-DE-LANCE

KEEL-BILLED TOUCAN

A SCARY SNAKE

The fer-de-lance is a poisonous snake that lives in Guatemala. Its fangs are nearly an inch long. Its bite can be deadly to animals and humans!

BLACK-HANDED
SPIDER MONKEY

Life Span: 22 years
Red List Status: endangered

black-handed
spider monkey range = ■

LEAST CONCERN	NEAR THREATENED	VULNERABLE	ENDANGERED	CRITICALLY ENDANGERED	EXTINCT IN THE WILD	EXTINCT

Over 15 million people live in Guatemala. Many Guatemalans are *mestizo,* with Maya and Spanish **ancestors**. Other Guatemalans have European **heritage**. Nearly two-fifths are direct **descendants** of **native** Maya groups. Groups such as the K'iche and Mam often live in small villages in Guatemala's western highlands.

Many Guatemalans belong to the Roman Catholic Church. Others are Protestant or practice other forms of Christianity. Some people also practice native Maya beliefs. More than two-thirds of Guatemalans speak Spanish, the nation's official language. Others speak various Mayan languages.

FAMOUS FACE

Name: Rigoberta Menchú
Birthday: January 9, 1959
Hometown: Chimel, Guatemala
Famous for: Winner of the 1992 Nobel Peace Prize for her work in support of human rights for the native people and low-income farmers of Guatemala and beyond

SPEAK SPANISH

ENGLISH	SPANISH	HOW TO SAY IT
hello	hola	OH-lah
goodbye	adiós	ah-dee-OHS
please	por favor	pohr fah-VOR
thank you	gracias	grah-SEE-ahs
yes	sí	SEE
no	no	noh

SUMPANGO

COMMUNITIES

Just over half of Guatemala's population live in **urban** areas. Almost 3 million people live in Guatemala City alone. Housing varies depending on wealth. Some live in apartments or fancy homes. But many homes are made of cardboard or other materials. Buses are a popular way to get around in the crowded cities.

GUATEMALA CITY

CORN HOUSES

More than 5 million Guatemalans live in homes made of cornstalk or cardboard walls. These are not very sturdy, especially during the rainy season.

In **rural** areas, families tend to stick together. Extended family members often share a **compound** with homes made of concrete or wood. People in the countryside often gather to socialize at local markets or churches.

Guatemalans are known for being polite and friendly.
They might greet each other by saying *mucho gusto*,
"pleased to meet you," or *buenos días*, "good day."
Men exchange a firm handshake when they meet.
Women commonly greet others with kisses on the cheeks.

In the cities, it is common to see Western-style clothing. But in rural areas, people often wear brightly colored, **traditional** clothing. Maya women may wear a *corte*, or a wraparound skirt. Both men and women wear a woven belt called a *faja*.

CLOTHES FROM HOME

Maya women often wear blouses called *huipils*. Designs on the huipils show where the women are from as well as their social status.

Students in Guatemala start six years of free primary school at age 6. Most finish primary school, but many do not move on to secondary school. They must work to support their families. But students who complete secondary school can study at universities.

More than half of Guatemala's workforce have **service jobs** in fields like banking or education. **Tourism** is also an important source of income. Nearly one-third of Guatemalans work in agriculture. Other people make products like clothing or furniture.

WEAVING

FARMERS

FEATHERS AS MONEY

Guatemala's national currency, the Guatemalan quetzal, is named after the beautiful quetzal bird. The ancient Maya used its feathers as currency.

Football, or soccer, is Guatemala's most popular sport. The national team plays all over the world. *Chamusca*, or street soccer, is played anywhere a group of people wants to start a match. Guatemalans also enjoy hiking and white-water rafting.

CHAMUSCA

People often spend time socializing with friends and family. In the cities, parks are filled with visitors. In the countryside, markets are a popular place to meet up and hang out with friends. For those who live near the coasts, Guatemala's beaches make nice getaways.

VOLLEYBALL

WORRY DOLL

What You Need:
- one pipe cleaner
- a large wooden or plastic bead
- permanent marker
- yarn
- scissors

Instructions:
1. Cut the pipe cleaner into two pieces. One of these pieces should be twice as long as the other. Bend each piece of cut pipe cleaner in half.

2. Gather some yarn strands together with a back-and-forth motion until you have a small pile. This will be the hair.

3. Draw a face on the bead using permanent marker. Place the yarn into the fold of the long pipe cleaner. The yarn and pipe cleaner should be interlocked.

4. Feed the bead over both ends of this pipe cleaner until it reaches the hair.

5. Twist the shorter pipe cleaner around the longer one to make arms.

6. Wind some yarn around the arms and legs of your doll. Tie it off when you are done. Tell your worries to your doll, and place it under your pillow!

GOOD MANNERS

Guatemalans keep their hands
above the table when eating.
It is considered good manners.

Most Guatemalans eat three meals each day, and each
meal often includes black beans, corn tortillas, and rice.
Eggs and fried plantains are common breakfast foods.
Lunch is the biggest meal of the day. Dishes like *pepián* are
common. *Pepián* is a spicy stew or sauce made with meat
and vegetables.

Another popular dish is *kak'ik*. This turkey soup is a traditional Maya dish. It includes many spices like chiles and coriander. Guatemalans also enjoy tropical fruits like papaya and breadfruit.

PEPIÁN

KAK'IK

CHAMPURRADAS RECIPE

Ingredients:

2 cups flour
3/4 cup sugar
2 teaspoons baking powder
10 tablespoons unsalted butter
pinch of salt
3 eggs
3 teaspoons vanilla extract
3-4 tablespoons sesame seeds
    (enough to sprinkle over the cookies)
cooking spray

Steps:

1. With an adult present, preheat the oven to 350 degrees Fahrenheit (177 degrees Celsius).

2. In a large bowl, combine the flour, sugar, baking powder, and salt.

3. Add two eggs, butter, and vanilla extract. Mix until all ingredients are combined and the dough is formed.

4. Using a tablespoon, scoop out 20 balls of dough. Place these about 2 inches (5 centimeters) apart on a greased cookie sheet. With your fingers, press the top of each cookie to flatten it.

5. In a small bowl, beat the remaining egg with a fork. Brush the top of each cookie with this egg yolk. Sprinkle sesame seeds over the top of the cookies.

6. Bake until the cookies are golden brown, about 20 minutes.

CELEBRATIONS

Many of Guatemala's biggest celebrations are Christian holidays. *Semana Santa*, or Holy Week, is the week leading up to Easter. The city of Antigua is known for its fancy floats and grand parades. People from all over Guatemala travel there to attend services at the Baroque-style San José Cathedral.

Guatemala celebrates its independence from Spain on September 15. Festivities across the country include dancing and firework displays. Marchers in colorful uniforms take part in parades all over the nation. But Guatemalans celebrate their country and **culture** all year long!

SEMANA SANTA

DAY OF THE DEAD

November 1 is *Día de los Muertos,* or
Day of the Dead. Families remember their
loved ones who have died by decorating
graves. They also fly kites to encourage
feelings of peace and to provide company
for the living.

1776
Guatemala City becomes the capital

1821
Guatemala gains independence from Spain

250–900 CE
Peak of the Maya civilization

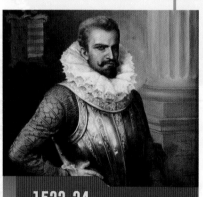

1941
Guatemala declares war on Axis powers during World War II

1523–24
Spanish explorer Pedro de Alvarado defeats the Maya and Guatemala becomes a Spanish colony

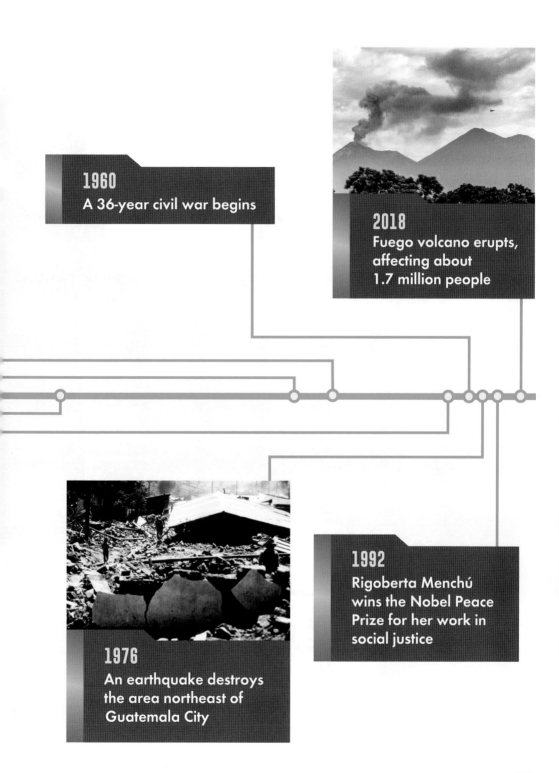

1960
A 36-year civil war begins

2018
Fuego volcano erupts,
affecting about
1.7 million people

1976
An earthquake destroys
the area northeast of
Guatemala City

1992
Rigoberta Menchú
wins the Nobel Peace
Prize for her work in
social justice

Official Name: Republic of Guatemala

Flag of Guatemala: Guatemala's flag has three vertical bands of color. The left and right bands are light blue, representing the Pacific Ocean and the Caribbean Sea. The central band is white. It symbolizes purity and peace. The country's coat of arms is in the middle of the white band. It includes the national bird, a wreath, a rifle, and two crossed swords. There is also a scroll showing the nation's date of independence.

Area: 42,042 square miles
(108,889 square kilometers)

Capital City: Guatemala City

Important Cities: Mixco, Villa Nueva, Petapa, Quetzaltenango

Population:
15,460,732 (July 2017)

COUNTRYSIDE
48.9%

WHERE
PEOPLE LIVE

CITY
51.1%

SERVICES
55.8%

JOBS

MANUFACTURING
12.8%

FARMING
31.4%

Main Exports:

sugar

coffee

petroleum

clothing

bananas

fruits and vegetables

National Holiday:
Independence Day (September 15)

Main Language:
Spanish

Form of Government:
presidential republic

Title for Country Leader:
president

RELIGION

PROTESTANT
40%

OTHER
2%

MAYA
1%

ROMAN CATHOLIC
57%

Unit of Money:
Guatemalan quetzal

GLOSSARY

ancestors—relatives who lived long ago

compound—an enclosed area that includes a group of buildings

culture—the beliefs, arts, and ways of life in a place or society

descendants—people related to a person or group of people who lived at an earlier time

gulf—part of an ocean or sea that extends into land

heritage—the traditions, achievements, and beliefs that are part of the history of a group of people

Maya—a native American people from the Yucatán Peninsula and neighboring areas

native—originally from the area or related to a group of people that began in the area

plateau—an area of flat, raised land

rural—related to the countryside

service jobs—jobs that perform tasks for people or businesses

tourism—the business of people traveling to visit other places

trade winds—winds blowing almost constantly in one direction

traditional—related to customs, ideas, or beliefs handed down from one generation to the next

tropical—related to the the tropics; the tropics is a hot, rainy region near the equator.

urban—related to cities and city life

volcanic—relating to a hole in the earth that erupts hot ash, gas, or melted rock called lava

TO LEARN MORE

AT THE LIBRARY

Hudak, Heather C. *A Refugee's Journey from Guatemala*. New York, N.Y.: Crabtree Publishing Company, 2018.

Sheehan, Sean, Magdalene Koh, and Alex Tessman. *Guatemala*. New York, N.Y.: Cavendish Square, 2018.

Spilsbury, Louise. *The Mayans*. UK: Raintree, 2017.

ON THE WEB

FACTSURFER

Factsurfer.com gives you a safe, fun way to find more information.

1. Go to www.factsurfer.com.

2. Enter "Guatemala" into the search box.

3. Click the "Surf" button and select your book cover to see a list of related web sites.

INDEX